Samuel Musgrave

The Musgrave controversy

Being a collection of curious and interesting papers on the subject of the

late peace

Samuel Musgrave

The Musgrave controversy
Being a collection of curious and interesting papers on the subject of the late peace

ISBN/EAN: 9783337226701

Printed in Europe, USA, Canada, Australia, Japan

Cover: Foto ©Thomas Meinert / pixelio.de

More available books at **www.hansebooks.com**

BEING

A COLLECTION OF.

CURIOUS AND INTERESTING PAPERS,

ON THE

SUBJECT OF THE LATE PEACE.

LONDON,

Printed for J. Miller, No. 2, Queen's-Head-Paffage, Newgate-ftreet; and fold by S. Bladon, No. 28, Paternofler-Row; F. Blyth, at the Royal Exchange; and J. Almon, Piccadilly.

PRICE ONE SHILLING.

COPY of the DEVONSHIRE INSTRUCTIONS.

To Sir RICHARD WARWICK BAMPFYLDE, Bart. and JOHN PARKER, Efq; Knights of the Shire for the County of DEVON.

WE, the Freeholders of the County of Devon, affembled in a General Meeting at the Caftle of Exon, find ourfelves called upon by many weighty confiderations to exercife the conftitutional and unqueftionable right of inftructing our Members with regard to their conduct in Parliament. It becomes now more highly neceffary, when an opinion has been publickly avowed, derogatory from that relation which ought to fubfift between the Electors and their Reprefentatives. We, therefore, enjoin you to promote and fupport an enquiry into all thofe grievances that have fo juftly alarmed the fubjects of this kingdom; particularly, for what reafons a magiftrate, in the immediate fervice of the Crown, to whom informations of the moft important nature were imparted by a native and Freeholder of this County, refufed to examine or enquire after the evidence pointed out to him; being a perfon the moft capable of clearing up the affair, both from his own knowledge, and the papers *then* in his poffeffion; in confequence of which refufal, fecrets of the moft important nature to the fafety of this kingdom have been probably loft, and the alledged inftruments of difhonour to his Majefty's government fcreen'd from cenfure and punifhment; and that you will diligently purfue an enquiry into the criminal tranfactions referred to in that information; and that you alfo ufe your utmoft endeavours to fhorten the duration of Parliaments.

Voted at the Caftle of Exon, Oct. 5, 1769.

THE

MUSGRAVE CONTROVERSY,

An ADDRESS *to the Gentlemen, Clergy, and Freeholders of the County of Devon, preparatory to the General Meeting at Exeter on Thurſday the 5th of October,* 1769.

By Dr. MUSGRAVE,

Phyſician at Plymouth.

GENTLEMEN,

THE Sheriff having ſummoned a meeting of the county in order to conſider of a Petition for redreſs of grievances, I think it incumbent on me as a lover of my country in general to lay before you a tranſaction, which, I apprehend, gives juſter grounds of complaint and apprehenſion than any thing hitherto made public. Having long had reaſon to imagine that the nation has been cruelly and fatally injured in a way which they little ſuſpect, I have ardently

B w.ſhed

wifhed for the day, when my imperfect information fhould be fuperfeded by evidence
and certainty. That day, I flatter myfelf,
is at laft approaching, and that the fpirit
which now appears among the Freeholders
will bear down every obftacle that may be
thrown in the way of open and impartial
enquiry.

I need not remind you, Gentlemen, of the
univerfal indignation and abhorrence, with
which the conditions of the late peace were
received by the independant part of the nation. Yet fuch is the candid, unfufpecting
nature of Englifhmen, that even thofe who
condemned the meafure did not attribute it
to any worfe motive than an unmanly impatience under the burdens of the war, and a
blind, headlong defire to be relieved from
them. They did not conceive that perfons
of high rank and unbounded wealth could be
feduced by gold to betray the interefts of their
country, and furrender advantages, which the
lives of fo many heroes had been willingly
facrificed to purchafe. Such a fuppofition,
unhappily for us, is at prefent far from in-
credible. The important fecret was difclofed
to me in the year 1764, during my refidence
at Paris. I will not trouble you with a detail of the intermediate fteps I took in the affair, which, however, in proper time I fhall
moft fully and readily difcover. It is fufficient to fay, on the 10th of May 1765, by
the direction of Dr. Backftone I waited on
Lord Halifax, then Secretary of State, and
                                    delivered

delivered to him an exact narrative of the intelligence I had received at Paris, with copies
of four letters to and from Lord Hertford.
The behaviour of Lord Halifax was polite
but evasive. When I pressed him in a second
interview to enquire into the truth of the
charge, he objected to all public steps that
might give an alarm, and asked me whether
I could point out to him any way of prose-
cuting the enquiry in secret, and whether in
so doing there was any probability of his ob-
taining positive proof of the fact. I was not
so much the dupe of his artifice as to believe
that he had any serious intention of following the clue I had given him, though his dif-
course plainly pointed that way. It appeared
by the sequel that I had judged right. For
having four days after given a direct and satis-
factory answer to both his questions, he then
put an end to my solicitations by a peremp-
tory refusal to take any steps whatever in the
affair.

It is here necessary to explain what I mean
by enquiring into the truth of the charge.
In the summer of the year 1764, an overture
had been made to Sir George Yonge, Mr.
Fitzherbert, and several other Members of
Parliament, in the name of the Chevalier
D'Eon, importing that he, the Chevalier,
was ready to impeach three persons, two of
whom are Peers and Members of the Privy
Council, of selling the peace to the French.
Of this proposal I was informed at different
times by the two gentlemen above-mentioned.

Sir

Sir **George** Yonge in particular told me that he underſtood the charge could be ſupported by written as well as living evidence. The ſtep that I urged Lord Halifax to take, was to ſend for the Chevalier D'Eon, to examine him upon the ſubject of this overture, to peruſe his papers, and then to proceed according to the proofs. In ſuch a caſe a more deciſive evidence than the Chevalier D'Eon could not be wiſhed for. He had the negociation on the part of the enemy, and was known to have in his poſſeſſion the diſpatches and papers of the Duke de Nivernois. This gentleman, ſo qualified and ſo diſpoſed to give light into the affair, did Lord Halifax refuſe to examine ; whether from an apprehenſion that the charge would not be made out, or on the contrary that it could. I leave you, gentlemen, and every impartial reader to judge.

It muſt not be underſtood, that I can myſelf ſupport a charge of corruption againſt the noble Lords named in my information. My complaint is of a different nature and againſt a different perſon. I conſider the refuſal of Lord Halifax as a willful obſtruction of national juſtice, for which I wiſh to ſee him undergo a ſuitable puniſhment. Permit me to obſerve, gentlemen, that ſuch an obſtruction not only gives a temporary impunity to offenders, but tends alſo to make that impunity perpetual, by deſtroying or weakening the proofs of their guilt. Evidence of all kinds is a very periſhable thing. Living

witneſſes

witnesses are expofed to the chance of mortality, and written evidence to the not uncommon cafualty of fire. In the prefent cafe fome-thing more than thefe ordinary accidents might with good reafon be apprehended. It ftands upon record that the Count de Guer-chy had confpired to affaffinate the Chevalier D'Eon, neither has this charge hitherto been refuted or anfwered. This not fucceeding, a band of ruffians was hired to kidnap that gen-tleman, and carry off his papers. Though this fecond attempt failed, it does not follow that thefe important papers are ftill fecure. I was informed by Mr. Fitzherbert, fo long ago as the 17th of May, 1765, that he had then intelligence of overtures making to the Che-valier D'Eon, the object of which was to get the papers out of his hands in return for a ftipulated fum of money. This account I communicated the following day to Lord Halifax, who ftill perfifted in expofing thofe precious documents to fo many complicated hazards. I fay precious documents, becaufe if they fhould be unfortunately loft, the affair muft be for ever involved in uncertainty, an uncertainty, gentlemen, which may be pro-ductive of infinite mifchiefs to the nation, and cannot tend to the advantage or fatisfaction of any but the guilty.

Lord Halifax, in excufe for his refufal, will probably alledge, as he did to me, his perfua-fion that the charge was wholly groundlefs. I need not obferve, how mifplaced and frivo-lous fuch an allegation is when applied to juftify

tify a magiftrate for not examining evidence.
But I will fuppofe for argument's fake the
perfons accufed to be perfectly innocent. Is it
not the intereft and the wifh of every innocent
man to have his conduct fcrutinized while
facts are recent, and truth, of confequence, eafy
to be diftinguifhed from falfhood? Is there
any tendernefs in fuffering a ftain to remain
upon their characters till it becomes difficult,
or even impoffible to be wiped out? Will therefore thefe noble perfons, if their actions have
been upright, will they, I fay, thank Lord
Halifax for depriving them of an early oppor-
of eftablifhing their innocence? Will they
not regret and execrate his caution, if the fubfequent fuppreffion or deftruction of the evidence fhould concur with other circumftances
to fix on them the fufpicion of guilt? How
will Lord Halifax excufe himfelf to his So-
vereign, for fuffering fo attrocious a calumny
to fpread and take root, to the evident hazard
of his royal reputation? And what amends will
he make to the nation for the heart burnings and
jealoufies which are the natural fruits of fuch
a procedure? Yet thefe, gentlemen, are the
leaft of the mifchiefs that may be apprehended from his behaviour upon the footing
of his own plea.

I will venture however to affert, that, as
far as hitherto appears, the weight of evidence and probability is on the contrary fide.
Now, fuppofing the charge to be true, there
can be no need of long arguments to convince
you of the injury done to the nation, by fuffering

fering fuch capital offenders to efcape. For
what is this but to defraud us of the only
compenfation we can expect for the lofs of
fo many important territories, a lofs rendered
ftill more grievous by the indignity of paying
a penfion, as we notorioufly do, to the foreign minifters who negociated the ruinous
bargain ? Yet even thefe confiderations are
infinitely out-weighed by the danger to which
the whole nation muft be expofed from the
continued operation of fo much authority, in-
fluence, and favour to their prejudice, and,
above all, from the poffibility that the fu-
preme government of the kingdom may, by
the regency-act, devolve to a perfon directly
and pofitively accufed of high treafon. Even
the encouragement that fuch an impunity
muft give to future treafons, is enough to fill
a thinking mind with the moft painful ap-
prehenfions. We live in an age, not greatly
addicted to fcruples, when the open avowal
of domeftic venality feems to lead men, by
an eafy gradation, to connexions equally
mercenary with foreigners and enemies. How
then can we expect ill-difpofed perfons to re-
fift a temptation of this fort, when they find
that treafon may be detected, and proofs of
it offered to a magiftrate, without producing
either punifhment or enquiry ? The confequence of this may be, our living to fee a
French party, as well as a court party, in
parliament; which, fhould it ever happen,
no imagination can fufficiently paint the ca-
lamitous and horrid ftate to which our late
glorious

glorious triumphs might finally be reduced.
When I talk of a French party in parliament,
I do not fpeak a mere vifionary language un-
fupported by experience. The hiftory of all
ages informs us, that France, where other
weapons have failed, has conftantly had re-
courfe to the lefs alarming weapons of in-
trigue and corruption. And how effectual
thefe have fometimes been, we have a recent
and tragical example in the total enflaving of
Corfica.

I have been thus particular in enumerating
the evils that may refult from the refufal of
Lord Halifax, not from a defire of aggravat-
ing that nobleman's offence, but merely to
evince the neceflity of a fpeedy enquiry, while
there is yet a chance of its not being wholly
fruitlefs. Though the courfe of my narrative has unavoidably led me to accufe his
Lordfhip, accufation is not my object, but
enquiry, which cannot be difagreeable to any
but thofe to whom truth itfelf is difagreeable.
In purfuing this point, I have hitherto been
fruftrated from the very circumftance which
ought to have infured my fuccefs, the im-
menfe importance of the queftion. It has
been apprehended, how juftly I know not,
that any magiftrate, who fhould commence
an enquiry, or any gentleman who fhould
openly move for it, would be deemed refpon-
fible for the truth of the charge, and fub-
jected to fevere penalties, if he could not
make it good. This imagination, however,
did not deter me, though fingle and unpro-
tected,

tected, from carrying my papers to the Speaker,
to be laid before the late Houfe of Commons.
The Speaker was pleafed to juftify my conduct, by allowing, that the affair ought to
be enquired into, but refufed at the fame
time to be inftrumental in promoting the enquiry himfelf. What then remained to be
done? What, but to wait, though with re-
luctance and impatience, till a proper opportunity fhould offer for appealing to the public
at large, that is, till the accumulated errors
of government fhould awaken a fpirit of enquiry too powerful to be refifted or eluded?
That this fpirit is now reviving, we have a
fufficient earneft in the unanimous zeal you
have fhewn for the appointment of a county
meeting. In fuch a conjuncture, to withold
from you fo important a truth, would no
longer be prudence, it would be to difgrace
my former conduct, it would fhew that I had
been actuated by fome temporary motives,
and not by a fteady and uniform regard to national good. Indeed, the declared purpofe of
your meeting is in itfelf a call upon every
freeholder to difclofe whatever you are concerned to know. I obey this call without
hefitation, fubmitting the profecution of the
affair to your judgment, in full confidence
that the refult of your deliberations will do
honour at the fame time to your prudence,
candour, and patriotifm.

Plymouth, Aug. 12, 1769.

C

Repenfe

Reponfe du Chevalier D'Eon a la lettre que M. le DOCTEUR MUSGRAVE *a fait imprimer dans le Public Advertifer du 2 Sept.* 1769, *No.* 10869, *& qui a enfuite ete copiee dans tous les autres papiers, fous la datte de Plymouth, le* 12 *Aout, &c.*

MONSIEUR,

VOUS me permettrez de croire que vous ne m'avez jamais plus connu, que je n'ai l'honneur de vous connoitre : & fi dans votre lettre du 12 Aout vous n'aviez pas abufe de mon nom, je ne me verrois pas force d'entrer en correfpondence avec vous.

Vous pretendez que " dans l'ete de 1764, " on fit des ouvertures en mon nom a dif- " ferens membres du parlement, portantes " que j'etois pret a accufer trois perfonnes, " donc deux etoient pairs, et membres au " confeil prive, d'avoir vendu la paix a la " France ;" & vous paroiffez fonder la deffus l'evidence de l'accufation, que vous dites en avoir porte vous memes a Milord Halifax.

Je vous declare en confequence ici Monfieur, que je n'ai jamais ni fait faire aucune ouverture pareille, ni dans l'hiver, ni dans l'ete de 1764, ni dans aucun tems. Je fuis d'une part trop fidele au miniftere que j'ai rempli, et de l'autre trop zelateur de la verite.

J'avoue que vous ne dites pas que ce foit moi qui aie fait ces propofitions : Mais feule-
ment

ment qu'elles ont ete fait en mon nom, fpecialement a M. le Chevalier George Yonge & a M. Fitzherbert.

Je vous affure ne connoitre aucun de ces Meffieurs & n'avoir jamais authorife qui que ce foit a faire, en mon nom, de pareilles ouvertures, que mon horreur feule pour la calomnie me feroit detefter.

Je vous interpelle donc, M. le Docteur, de declarer au public le nom du temeraire qui s'eft fervi du mien pour faire ces ouvertures odieufes. Ces Meffieurs que vous avez denonce comme vos temoins, ne peuvent vous refufer de venger leur veracite & la votre.

Quoique je ne puiffe m'empecher de louer votre droiture qui cite fes auteurs, cependant il me paroit de la derniere imprudence, dans une affaire d'une pareille gravite, de vous fonder fur un raport pour nommer publiquement un homme de mon caractere, fans l'avoir auparavant confulte. Si vous vous etiez fouvenu du dementi que j'ai donne dans le S. James's Chronicle du 25 Octobre 1766, No. 881, a un avertiffement du meme papier, No. 875, qui portoit en fubftance ce que vous alleguez dons votre derniere lettre, vous m'auriez epargne la peine de vous repondre aujourdhui. Qu'en va-t-il arriver ? Le public aura lu avidement votre lettre, aura ajoute foi a fon contenu parceque vous en appellez a mon evidence : Mais qu'en penfera t-il maintenant ? quand votre interet, mon honneur & la verite m'obligent a nier ce que vous y avancez a mon fujet.

Il

Il en eſt de meme de ce que vous pretendez
que " vers le 17 Mai 1765, M. Fitzherbert
" vous auroit dit ſavoir qu'on m'avoit fait des
" propoſitions de vendre pour une ſomme
" d'argent les papiers qui etoient entre mes
" mains."

Je me ſuis toujours flatte de l'eſtime & de
l'amitie des Anglois avec leſquels j'ai vecu.
Qui d'eux dans ces ſentimens auroit oſe me
temoigner aſſez de mepris pour me faire une
pareille propoſition ? L'injure m'en auroit ete
d'autant plus ſenſible que le caractere de la
perſonne auroit ete plus reſpectable.

Je ne vous ſuivrai, Monſieur, ni dans les
demarches que vous avez cru devoir faire, ni
dans les raiſonnemens dont vous vous ſervez
pour les appuier : Ceux-ci montrent l'orateur
& celles-la, ſi elles ſont fondees, preuvent le
patriote. Mais je vous atteſte ici, ſur ma
parole d'honneur & a la face du public, que
je ne puis vous etre d'aucune utilite, que je
ne ſuis jamais entre en marche pour la vente
de mes papiers, & que je n'ai jamais, ni par
moi-meme ni par aucun agent autoriſe de ma
part, propoſe de fait voir que la paix avoit ete
vendue a la France.

Si Milord Halifax, ou l'orateur, auxquels
vous dites vous etre addreſſe pour m'appeller
en temoignage ſur la validite de votre accuſa-
tion, m'avoient fait citer ; ils auroient connu
par mes reponſes que je penſe que l'Angleterre a plutot donne de l'argent a la France,
que la France de l'or a l'Angleterre pour conclure la derniere paix et que le bonheur que

j'ai

j'ai eu de concourir au falutaire ouvrage de cette paix m'a infpire les fentimens de la plus jufte veneration pour les commiffaires Anglois qui y ont ete emploies, & ceux de la plus vive eftime & de la plus fincere admiration pour feu M. le Comte de Viry qui, par fon attachement pour le bien des deux nations belligerantes & graces a fon zele infatiguable, eut la gloire d'amener cette paix neceffaire aux deux nations a une heureufe conclufion. Jugez maintenant, Monfieur, avec quelle folidite vous pouvois vous fonder fur moi pour rendre votre accufation evidente !

Je fuis trop connu en Angleterre pour avoir eu befoin de cette reponfe, fi la franchife de votre lettre me n'avoit paru meriter que je vous empechaffe de faire des demarches ulterieures qui ne pouroient tourner qu'a votre prejudice, puis qu'elles ne feroient fondees que fur de faux raports de mes actions. Pour vous mettre a meme d'etre auffi prudent que patriote, je figne cette lettre & vous y donne mon addreffe, afin que, pour foutenir votre veracite, vous me donniez les moiens de convaincre publiquement les calomniateurs, qui ont ofe fe fervir de mon nom, d'une maniere plus contraire encore a la verite des faits, qu'a la dignite avec lequelle, J'ai toujours foutenu mon caractere au millieu meme de la perfecution de mes enemis.

J'ai l'honneur d'etre votre tres humble ferviteur, LE CHEVALIER D'EON.

In Petty-France, Weftminfter,
    4 Septembre, 1769.

                    Tranflation

Tranflation of the Chevalier D'Eon's *Anfwer
to* Dr. Mufgrave's *Addrefs.*

S I R,

YOU will permit me to believe that
you never knew any more of me, than
I have the honour of knowing of you : and if
in your letter of the 12th of Auguft you had
not made a wrong ufe of my name, I fhould
not now find myfelf obliged to enter into a
correfpondence with you.

You pretend that " in the fummer of the
" year 1764, overtures were made in my
" name to feveral members of parliament,
" importing that I was ready to impeach
" three perfons, two of whom were peers
" and members of the privy council, of
" having fold the peace to the French :" and
you feem to found thereupon the evidence of
a charge, which you fay you carried yourfelf
to Lord Halifax.

I declare, therefore, here, Sir, that I never
made, nor caufed to be made any fuch overture, either in the winter or fummer of the
year 1764, nor at any other time : I am,
on one fide, too faithful to the office I
filled, and on the other too zealous a friend
to truth.

I confefs you do not fay it was I that made
thefe overtures ; but only that they were
made

made in my name, particularly to Sir George
Yonge and Mr. Fitzherbert.

I assure you I do not know either of these
gentlemen, and never authorised any person
whatever to make in my name such overtures, which the abhorrence alone I have
for calumny, would make me detest.

I call upon you, therefore, Sir, to lay before the public the name of the audacious
person who has made use of mine to cover
his own odious offers. The gentlemen whom
you have given as your witnesses, cannot deny
you this justification of their own veracity
and your's.

Though I cannot but commend your integrity in citing your authors, yet it appears
to me an act of the last imprudence, in an
affair of so much weight, to build upon report, for naming publickly a person of my
character, without having previously con-
sulted him. If you had recollected the con-
tradiction I gave in the St. James's Chronicle
of Oct. 25, 1766, No. 881, to an advertise-
ment in the same paper, No. 875, importing
in substance what you alledge in your last
letter, you had saved me the trouble of re-
plying to you at this time. What must be
the result ? The public will have read greed-
ily your letter ; will have believed it's contents, because you appeal therein to my
testimony : but what will they think now
when your own interest, my honour and
truth oblige me to deny all that you have
advanced thereon with respect to me.

It

It is the fame with your pretence that
" about the 17th of May, 1765, Mr. Fitz-
" herbert told you, he knew that overtures
" had been made to me to fell for a fum
" of money the papers that were in my
" hands.

I have always flattered myfelf with being
poffeffed of the efteem and friendfhip of the
Englifh with whom I have lived. Who of
them then in thefe fentiments would have
prefumed to have fhewn fufficient contempt
for me to have made me fuch an overture ?
The injury would have been the more fenfi-
bly felt by me, as the character of the perfon
was more refpectable.

I fhall not follow you, Sir, either in all the
fteps you have thought it your duty to take,
or in the arguments you made ufe of to fupport them : thefe fhew the orator, and thofe,
if they be well founded, prove the patriot.

But I here certify to you, on my word of
honour, and in the face of the public, that I
cannot be of any fort of ufe to you ; that
I never entered into any treaty for the fale of
my papers, and never either by myfelf or any
agent authorifed on my part, offered to make
appear, that the peace had been fold to
France.

If Lord Halifax, or the Speaker, to whom
you fay you addreffed yourfelf in order to
call upon me as evidence, with refpect to the
validity of your charge, had caufed me to be
cited, he might have known by my anfwers
what my thoughts were, that England rather

gave

gave money to France than France to England, to conclude the laft peace; and that the happinefs I had in concurring to the great work of peace has infpired me with fentiments of the jufteft veneration for the Englifh commiffioners who had been employed in it, and with the moft lively efteem and fincereft admiration for the late Count de Viry, who in his attachment to the welfare of the two nations then at war, and thanks to his indefatigable zeal! had the glory of bringing that peace to a happy conclufion.

Judge now, Sir, with what folidity you can depend upon me to make your charge clear.

I am too well known in England to have been under any neceffity of this reply, if the franknefs of your letter had not appeared to me to merit my preventing you from taking any further fteps, which could not but turn to your prejudice, in as much as they would be founded folely on falfe reports of *my* proceedings.

In order to enable you to be as prudent as patriotic, I fign this letter, and therein give you my addrefs, that for the maintenance of your own veracity you may furnifh me with the means of convicting publickly thofe flanderers who have dared to make ufe of my name, in a manner ftill more repugnant to real facts, than the dignity with which I have ever fupported my character.

I have the honour of being your moft humble fervant, *The Chevalier* D'EON.

In Petty France, Weftminfter.

To

To Charles-Genevieve-Louis-Augufte-Andre-Timothee D'Eon de Beaumont, *Chevalier de l'ordre roial & militaire de S. Louis,* * *Miniftre Plenipotentiare de France aupres du Roi de la Grande Bretagne, Captaine de Dragons au fervice de fa Majefte tres Chretienne, Avocat au Parlement de Paris, Cenfeur roial pour l'Hiftoire et les Belles Lettres en France, &c.*

L E T T E R I.

S I R,

I HAVE read with particular attention your letter to Dr. Mufgrave, and can no longer be in doubt what your bufinefs at prefent is in a country where you are an *outlaw.*

You exhibit to us a character moft fingularly profligate. You alone in this age have had it in your power to be equally falfe and treacherous to two fuch great nations as England and France. While you were only fecretary to the Duke of Nivernois, you abufed the privileges of your character, and engaged in the dirty bufinefs of *debauching our manufacturers.* You fo entirely forgot the dignity of your rank afterwards, when Minifter Plenipotentiary, that you continued the fame practice, although it is contrary to the law of nations. You do not even blufh to charge this article of expence in the ftate of your

* The Chevalier D'Eon began in this manner the affidavit he made Dec. 28, 1764, although his public character had been fuperfeded by the French King, and declared at an end by the King of England, above a year before.

.dif-

diſburſements to the Comte de Guerchy. "Avance aux ouvriers Anglois de la manu- "facture de toiles peintes, tant hommes que "femmes, debauche par le Sieur *L'Eſcalier* "a Londres et des environs pour les faire "paſſer ailleurs 195l." Lettres, Memoires, "&c. p. 172. The meanneſs and raſcality of ſuch an employment in you and Monſieur *L'Eſcalier* can only be equalled by the tame- neſs and ignominy of the adminiſtration at that time in ſuffering *L'Eſcalier,* a notorious pimp and an *outlaw* here, to be after this in the public character of *Secretary* of the Comte de Guerchy. The atteſtations of *L'Eſcalier*'s *outlawry* were printed here, witneſſed by So- lomon Schomberg, a Notary Public, and by the Lord Mayor. They were diſperſed at the Hague, to ſerve the purpoſe of ſhewing at a certain juncture that England was bullied by France. You afterwards quarrelled with all your beſt friends, as well as with the miniſters of your fortune, and your own Court, which had raiſed you ſo rapidly from nothing, from being a writer to the police at Paris on the pen- ſion of 600 livres, or 25 guineas a year, to the dignity of Miniſter Plenipotentiary at the moſt important Court in Europe. Modern times ſcarcely produce an inſtance of political treachery equal to your's in printing the ſe- crets of the Court by whom you were em- ployed, and the private letters of your bene- factor the Duke of Nivernois, of Monſieur Sainte-Foy, Monſieur Moreau, &c. Your particular quarrel with Guerchy had nothing

to do with the fentiments of the Duke of
Nivernois, of Meff. Sainte-Foy, Moreau, and
other gentlemen, on the conduct of the
French parliament, the adminiftration of
their finances, &c. which were intrufted to
you, as their private friend, under the feal of
fecrecy. You betrayed their confidence without the leaft provocation on their part, or a
pretence of juftification of your own conduct from any one circumftance in thofe letters. After quarrelling with almoft all your
own countrymen, you publifhed in the fame
volume a grofs abufe of this nation, and called the Englifh a parcel of fools and mad-
men, at the very time that this country af-
forded you an honourable protection, and
an hofpitality you have abufed. " Apres
" deux fecouffes de tremblement de terre, qui
" arriverent ici en 1750, *un foldat enthoufiafte*
" s'avifa d'en predire un troifieme, qui de-
" voit renverfer Londres. Il fe dit infpire,
" & d'un ton enthoufiafte en fixa le jour,
" l'heure, & la minute. Londres confterne
" au fouvenir des deux fecouffes qui s'etoient
" fuivies dans l'intervalle d'un mois, & plus
" effraie encore a l'approache d'un troifieme
" & plus terrible tremble mentque ce foldat
" enthoufiafte avoit annonce pour le 5 d'Avril,
" la ville s'eft montree fufceptible de toutes
" fortes d'impreffions. Plus de 50 mille ha-
" bitans, fur la foi de cet oracle, avoient ce
" jour-la pris la fuite : la plupart de ceux
" que les raifonnemens ou les raillerie de
" leurs amis avoient retenue, attendoient
" en

" en tremblant l'inftant critique, & n'ont
" montre de courage qu'apres qu'il a ete
" paffe. Le jour arrive, la prophetie, fem-
" blable a la plupart des predictions, ne fut
" point accomplie ; le faux Samuel fut mis
" un peu tard aux petites maifons & *la tete*
" *de ces fiers infulaires fi fenfes & fi philofophes ne*
" *fut pas a l'epreuve de la prophetie d'un fou.*"
P. 14. I believe there is not to be found fo
grofs and filly an abufe of a whole nation
for the weaknefs of a few hyfteric women,
and fuperannuated men, nor fo falfe a repre-
fentation of any fact. Were your other dif-
patches to your court, Sir, compofed of fuch
wretched ftuff as this ? I hope the *botile-con-
jurer* finds his place in the fecond part of
your *memoires.* That innocent joke of the
late Duke of Montague, your countrymen
generally talk and write of as a ferious proof
of the folly and credulity of this nation.
The Englifh laughed at your weak attack on
them as a nation, and fuperior to fuch a-
bufe, defired that you might continue to en-
joy the protection of their noble fyftem of
laws, and the privileges of their country.
They confidered their own glory, not the
worthleffnefs of the individual. They would
have parted with fo infignificant a wretch
as you without the leaft regret ; but they
would not fuffer you to be forced away,
nor kidnapped, merely becaufe it would
have been an outrage to their laws, and
the honour of their nation. They too,
as politicians, thought you might be induced to make fome difcoveries, and were ready

dy to profit by your treafon to your own
country in the fecrets you might reveal for
the benefit of their's, but at the fame time
they would have abhorred the traitor. When
I mention the Englifh nation as anxious for
your fafety, I mean the body of the people.
The adminiftration *at that time* wifhed that
you might be carried off to France. Mans-
field and Norton faw Guerchy often on the
occafion, and Sandwich figned more than
one warrant to apprehend you. The French
miniftry, and the people here in power at
that time, planned your deftruction; but
the generofity of two or three individuals
faved you, and preferved a viper in the bo-
fom of their country. Now is juft the fea-
fon for fuch noxious reptiles to come forth.
They always meet the approaching ftorm.
Leagued with the enemies of our country,
whether French or Englifh, your flender a-
bilities are ftill employed againft a nation
you hate, but in your heart honour and re-
vere. After having for fome years talked
very openly of the wonderful difcoveries you
could make, and the impeachment you
could fupport, after frequently declaring,
that *you had two heads in your pocket*, when a
worthy gentleman fteps forth and ftates the
charge, you at once recoil, and declare that
you do not even believe a word of it, but
think that *l'Angleterre a plutot donne de l'argent
a la France, que la France de l'or a l'Angleterre
pour conclure la derniere paix.* So abfurd an
idea I fhall not undertake to refute, becaufe
I believe you are the only man *at large*, who
entertains

entertains it; but I shall in this first addrefs to you, defire you to ftate *two* facts to the public, relative to the fubject of your letter to Dr. Mufgrave. The *first* is, What was the negociation relative to the ifland of *Porto-Rico*? The Duke of Bedford fet out for Paris, Sept. 5, 1762. Every thing of importance was foon entirely fettled between the two courts. The moft material arrangements had been made here in private with Lord Bute before his Grace's departure. The news of the taking the Havannah was afterwards firft received in England, while the Duke was in Paris, on Sept. 29. Now I afk what alteration in the terms of the treaty did fuch important intelligence produce? What was to be given England, additional to the former ftipulations, in confequence of the furrender of the Havannah, when that likewife was to be given up? You are called upon to ftate that tranfaction; what you know of the ten days ceffion of Porto Rico to us by the negociation at Paris, and the fubfequent furrender of that ifland on the receipt of *two* letters from hence, one of which the Duke of Bedford ought to produce for his juftification in *that part* of the bufinefs; the other is too facred to appear. The *fecond* queftion I shall now afk is, *whether you have not declared that you were offered* 7000 *louis for your papers?* Your letter to Dr. Mufgrave is extremely evafive on this head. You fay, " Je me fuis toujours flatte de l'eftime & de " l'amitie *des Anglois* avec lefquels j'ai vecu,

" *Qui d'eux* dans ces fentimens auroit ofe me
" temoigner affez de mepris pour me faire
" une pareille propofition ?" No, Sir, *no En-glifhman* was employed in fo dirty a bufinefs ;
but one of your own country was found to
make the propofition, to which you objected.
You faid the fum was too trifling for papers
of fuch importance. My other letters fhall
give the world more truths ; for I will drag
you forth to the public view, not merely as
a trifling Frenchman, trifling in every thing
ferious, and ferious only in trifles, but as
the enemy of England, as a penfioned tool
of a wicked miniftry, who hope by your
means to trifle or perplex an enquiry, which
may not ftop at your patron, the detefted
Thane, to whom, although a Frenchman,
you have facrificed the great *Sully* in the moft
fulfome and lying of all dedications, prefixed
to your pirated *Confiderations Hiftoriques & Po-litiques fur les Impos.*

Your connections, Sir, are at length dif-covered, and the plan of your operations, fo
fecretly concerted by Bute's three deputies,
Jenkinfon, Dyfon, and *Target* Martin, at a
houfe in Pall Mall, which governs this king-dom, fhall be given to the public. You will
experience, that although Englifh genero-fity makes us always ready to give refuge and
protection to a diftreffed foreigner, even from
the country of our inveterate enemies, we
will not fuffer among us a French traitor
and a fpy, in the pay of an adminiftration
odious

(27)

odious to this whole nation. I ſhall only at
preſent add, that one of your friends will
ſoon prove to you that your own poet *Cor-
neille* ſays very truly,

Et meme avec juſtice on peut trahir un traitre.

I am, Sir,

An ENGLISHMAN.

Sept. 11, 1769.

L E T T E R   II.

To the Chevalier D'Eon.

S I R,

THE warm applauſe you give to the
peace of Paris, and the negociators of
it, both Engliſh and French, did not in the
leaſt ſurpriſe me. You were well paid for it
at the time, and the private advantages derived to you from it did not ceaſe with its
ratification. The peace itſelf was in its own
nature ſo infamous, and ſo peculiarly *felonious*
to this country, which it robbed of almoſt
all its noble conqueſts, that no Engliſhman
was judged proper to be ſent with the authentic ratification of ſuch a French bargain.
It was given to you *contre toute regle & contre
toute uſage*, as the Duke de Praſlin ſays in your
Memoires; and the Duke of Nivernois ob-
ſerves in a letter to the Duke of Bedford,

E   that

that it was *une galanterie de votre miniftere, &
une bonte du Roi votre maitre, qui fe fert avec
plaifir* D'UN FRANCOIS *pour cette tournure.*
Befides, at the very time of the negociation
you held the Ambaffador's pen; and altho'
you were never entrufted with the moft important fecrets between the two courts, you
were employed in the revifal of that fatal in-
ftrument which tore from our bleeding war-
riors the fruits of all their victories, the greateft
acquifitions your rival nation had ever made.
You are allowed to have much chicanery;
and the tricking article about the Canada Bills
was the effect of your duping the Duke of
Bedford, and the good-humoured Mr. Neville.
You may therefore with reafon fpeak of the
peace of Paris in terms of rapture, as a
Frenchman, and as the Duke of Nivernois's
fecretary. I will ever mention it with indignation; for I am an Englifhman, and have
not that load of guilt to expiate to my
country, the advifing, making, or *approving*
fo ruinous a meafure. You are, however,
Sir, by no means fingular in your opinion of
the late *peace* even in this nation. We too
have many traitors among us. A fet of gentlemen at Weftminfter gave an *entire approbation* of the *preliminary articles,* even with the
very extraordinary original claufe about the
Eaft-India Company among them. Their
bankers beft know how that *approbation* was
obtained; but their fucceffors, altho' care-
lefs about the national debt, have had the
prudence as well as forefight for themfelves,
to

to pay off all debts contracted on that account.

You speak with some degree of modesty
concerning yourself when you mention the
peace of Paris, as if conscious that you had
only been employed to toll the bell for the
funeral of England's departed glory and
fame. When you mention Count *Viry*,
you are quite lavish in his praises, knowing
how much he had been a principal in that
accursed treaty. I respect the dead; but
only the departed virtuous and good. I di-
stinguish characters, notwithstanding the
trite maxim of *de mortuis nil nisi bonum*. I
will never confound a Cato and a Cataline,
but will give to each their due. I execrate
the memory of Count Viry, as the enemy of
my country, as having been a principal in
robbing England of the *Havannah*, Porto
Rico, *Martinique, Guadelupe, Desiderade, Ma-
riegalante, St. Peter, Miquelon, Goree, Belleisle,
St. Lucia, &c.* and negociating a treaty
which has proved the salvation of France. I
believe you have, besides the general cause of
the peace, which saved France, two particular reasons for the regard you testify to the
memory of Count Viry. The first is the
very dexterous management he used to get
the claim of a sugar island from France
waved, in which you knew she was ready to
have acquiesced. The other is, the protest
he signed in favour of the House of Savoy,
which he procured to be legally attested and
given in at the time of the last coronation, in

the

the name of his mafter, the prefent King of
Sardinia. He too in your time had printed
the *Genealogie de la Famille Royale d'Angleterre*,
by which he hoped at a future day that the
ridiculous claims of his mafter's family, as
being, although Papifts, immediately defcended from Henrietta Maria, the daughter
of Charles I. would have prevailed over
thofe of the Houfe of Brunfwick, who are
defcended from Elizabeth, Electrefs Palatine, one degree more remote from the
Crown, as being the daughter of James I.
You both expected at leaft a general confufion
fpeedily among us; but neither you, nor he,
born under arbitrary governments, could
have any idea of the only lawful right to the
crown of thefe realms, a parliamentary right.
The contrary doctrine was in Queen Anne's
time exprefly declared to be *high treafon*,
by a particular ftatute, the " Act for the
" better fecuring her Majefty's perfon and
" government, and the fucceffion to the
" crown of England in the proteftant line ;"
That if any perfon or perfons, from and after the
25th day of March 1706, fhall malicioufly, ad-
vifedly and directly, by writing or printing, de-
clare, maintain, or affirm that the Kings or Queens
of England, with and by the authority of the par-
liament of England, are not able to make laws and
ftatutes of fufficient force and validity to limit and
bind the crown of this realm, and the DESCENT,
LIMITATION, INHERITANCE, *and govern-*
ment thereof, every fuch perfon or perfons fhall be
guilty of High Treafon, and being thereof con-
victed

victed and attainted, &c. &c. Count Viri acted
by the exprefs orders of his Court, in conjuction with your's. In the fame manner
the two Courts acted in concert at the beginning of this century, in the laft year of
our glorious Deliverer, King William III.
Count Maffei, the Ambaffador from Savoy,
delivered in the firft famous proteftation, in
the name of the Duchefs of Savoy, againft
the Hanover fucceffion, at the time the Duke
himfelf commanded the French army in
Italy, with Marfhal Catinat and the Prince
of Vaudemont under him, and every action
of his life was dictated by France. I believe
you therefore *unufually* fincere, when you
exprefs, " la plus vive eftime & la plus fin-
" cere admiration pour feu Monfieur le
" Comte de Viry, qui par fon attachement
" pour le bien des deux nations belligerantes
" & graces a fon zele infatiguable, eut la
" gloire d'amener cette paix neceffaire aux
" deux nations a une heureufe conclufion."
What this *happy conclufion* for England was,
we have already feen. From that fatal moment France, like a tall bully, began again
to lift the head, and infult all its neighbours.
You tell Dr. Mufgrave, " le public aura
" lu avidement votre lettre, aura adjute
" foi a fon contenu parceque vous en appel-
" lez a mon evidence." You are miftaken.
Your evidence of itfelf will have little weight
with any one, but you may have papers of
importance, which the public expected from
your own abfolute promife. The laft page of
your

your tirefome quarto promifed a fecond volume on the firft of June 1764, and a third
the firft of September. You ought to have
given them at the ftipulated time, and to
have made them as valuable as you could
from the materials of others, were it only to
indemnify us for having waded through the
family dullnefs and impertinence of the letters to your mother, nurfe, &c. &c. What
did the Scot give you for the fuppreffion ?
Was it as much as you had for the dedica-
tion, in which you tell him that you find
" dans les portraits du Duc de Sully & de
" Milord Bute une reffemblance affez par-
" faite, de grandes vertus, l'amour de la
" patrie (*Scotland I fuppofe*) de la philofophie;
" la profondeur d'un politique, l'eloquence
" d'un homme d'etat, cette aĉtivite d'efprit
" pui donne les fucces & les revers, ce coup
" d'œil qui demele les objets meme au milieu
" du trouble, qui fait le grand negociateur,
" &c. &c." Upon my word you merited the
whole fum he gave you, let it have been
ever fo confiderable. But did you believe
one fingle feature of *Bute* was like *Sully?* I
am fatisfied no more than your mafter the
Duke of Nivernois, Ambaffador and Acade-
mician, one of your *quarante immortels*, believed that the Kings of England and France
were *faits pour s'aimer, formed to love each
other,* although he declared fo at St. James's
with the utmoft gravity, and afterwards
printed it, like a compliment of the French
Academy, only in both French and Englifh
for

for the amufement of the two nations. The flattery of the French ambaſſador and fecre-tary ſucceeded. The Engliſh monarch and his Scottiſh miniſter were equally captivated; and the moſt gallant army in Europe were left to regret that they had not once the honour even of a viſit from our ſovereign during the whole war, or before they were diſbanded. The early and dangerous intrigues, the ſpe-cious flattery of a home favourite, and an in-ſinuating foreign miniſter, but above all the holding out in ſuch terms, *le charactère dif-tinctif d'une bonne foi non equivoque,* at which the King of Pruſſia has ſo much laughed, lulled aſleep all heroiſm, ſuſpicion, and even curioſity.

You are very juſt, Sir, in the obſervation, that the public read with great eagerneſs Dr. Muſgrave's letter. The reaſon is plain. The fact, that French gold made the laſt peace, was long ago believed ; but the public re-joiced when a man of Dr. Muſgrave's un-blemiſhed reputation ſtated the preſumptive evidence in general terms to his countrymen of Devonſhire, becauſe then it ſeemed im-poſſible any longer to ſtifle the enquiry. You ſay, " Je vous interpelle donc, M. le Doc-" teur, de declarer au public le nom du te-" meraire qui s'eſt ſervi du mien pour faire " ces ouvertures odieuſes." The Doctor does not ſay that he ever heard the name of the perſon, who, *in your name,* applied to Sir George Yonge, Mr. Fitzherbert, and ſeve-ral other members of parliament. He only

declares

declares that Sir George Yonge and Mr. Fitzherbert informed him *at different times* that
an overture had been made IN THE NAME *of
the Chevalier d'Eon, importing that he, the
Chevalier, was ready to impeach three perfons,
two of whom are peers and members of the
privy council, of felling the peace to the French.*
Why do you not make your appeal to thefe
two gentlemen ? If neither of the placemen
fhould chufe to anfwer, if they are either
fearful or falfe, if the *boards of admiralty and
trade* have exacted at leaft a promife of fecrecy, I will name a third perfon to you, a
character unexceptionable, of a candour, pro-
bity, and honour equal to Dr. Mufgrave's,
fuperior I believe never exifted. I mean
Thomas Cholmondeley, Efq; the late mem-
ber for Chefhire, a relation of Lord Chatham. My reafon for naming this gentleman
you will fee in the following paffage. " It
" is true *(Pitt)* affifted in the firft debate
" upon General Warrants in 1764 ; but find-
" ing that fome of the party were in earneft
" in their defigns of going farther, and had
" prepared a motion againft the feizure of
" papers, which was, in fact, the great
" grievance ; and alfo finding that the *fa-*
" *vourite* dreaded the minority gaining a
" victory, left the party fhould be afterwards
" turned againft him ; and that the *favourite*
" had therefore fupported the adminiftration
" with all his might upon this occafion,
" the great patriot fcandaloufly withdrew
" from the caufe and the party ; thereby
" *preventing*

" *preventing* any point being then gained
" towards that fecurity of public liberty,
" which the whole kingdom fo ardently
" wifhed for and expected. A fhort time
" afterwards, when an IMPEACHMENT
" OF THE FAVOURITE was privately ru-
" moured among a few only ; and it was
" faid, that there was ftrong evidence ready
" to be given, *particularly with regard to the*
" *peace* ; when a certain baronet, and others,
" who took fome pains in order to come at
" this evidence, and the conditions upon
" which it might have been obtained were
" trifling, not pecuniary *(the pardon of the*
" *Chevalier D'Eon is here meant)* and who
" thought it neceffary that the great Com-
" moner fhould be confulted upon a fubject
" of fuch importance, efpecially too as he
" was looked upon to be the fitteft perfon to
" lead, or principally fupport fuch a pro-
" cedure ; and when, in confequence of that
" idea, he was applied to by one of his own
" friends, and, in fome meafure, a diftant
" relation, he checked the whole in the bud,
" by declaring vehemently againft it." *An
enquiry into the conduct of the late Right Honourable Commoner*, page 26, &c. publifhed
in 1766. The ftrange phrafe *Pitt* ufed was,
*that he would fet his foot on the head of the
man who firft moved the enquiry, and crufh him
to atoms.* I am very glad to hear that the
three brothers are at laft united, and that
there is now not only a family, but a political union among them. I venture however
F to

to prophefy, that two of the three will never promote an enquiry into the tranfactions of the laft *peace*, or the conduct of the *favourite*, and I therefore hope all the friends of the public will be on their guard againft them both. They cannot fafely be trufted with the conduct of this important bufinefs. The *apoftate* had in 1764 his peerage and place of Privy Seal in view, for which he then fold his friends and his country. He now looks forwards to a more lucrative office, a larger penfion to recruit his fhattered finances, and perhaps to a higher title, which he may probably get, if he can keep the favourite's head on his fhoulders. I wifh however the *triumvirate* of brothers fuccefs, becaufe I think a *triumvirate*, which fhould be only infolent and overbearing, is infinitely to be preferred to a fole minifter who is cruel, and *delights in blood*.

I fhould before this, Monfieur le Chevalier, have apologized to you for the franknefs of my proceeding with refpect to you, and the plain language of my heart, but really my nature is open and undifguifed. I detest flattery and foolifh compliments. I call things generally by their names, *j'appelle un chat un chat, et rolet un fripon*. Befides your example ought to weigh in an addrefs to you. The embaffador extraordinary and plenipotentiary of your court, a Cordon Bleu, who reprefented the perfon of the Moft Chriftian King, you repeatedly in the groffeft manner call *anc extraordinaire*, and you add, *la truye*

truye n'enoblit pas le cochon. Monfieur Buffy, the late French minifter here, is with you a *burreau.* Your language even to your own mother is particularly rude. You advife a tender affectionate parent, in tears for the mifconduct of a fon fhe loved, to *wipe her eyes, plant her cabbages, weed her garden, eat her greens, and drink the milk of her cows and the wine of her vineyard,* without giving herfelf any trouble about you. The letter to your nurfe, Madame Benoit a Tonnerre, is rather more obliging. You talk of all her *foins et peines paffees,* and then very elegantly add, that *you are well at prefent, but fhould be better if you could fee her foon.* To her you act the *fignor magnifico;* you actually fend her one hundred livres, or near four pounds and eight fhillings fterling. How interefting is all this to the public? how glorious to you? But to return to your poor mother, whom I heartily pity. You tell her in return for her concern, that you have read *toutes les lettres lamentables et pitoyables que vous avez pris la peine de m'ecrire: pourquoi pleurez vous, femme de peu de foi?* You make ufe here, Sir, of our Bleffed Saviour's words in a very ftrange and indecent manner. You fpeak of him in your laft publication, *in a moft daring and really impudent ftile.* In the *Pieces Authentiques,* page 13, your words are, *on n'accufa point Jefus Chrift au Banc d'Herode d'avoir debite des libelles; cependant ce que notre feigneur a avance n'a jamais ete fi bien prouve que ce que le Chevalier D'Eon a demontre par fes* LETTRES ET MEMOIRES.

Jefus

Jefus Chrift was not accufed at Herod's Bench of having publifhed libels ; although what our Saviour advanced was never fo well proved as what the Chevalier D'Eon has demonftrated in his Letters and Memoirs. After all thefe inftances I fhall conclude without the leaft compliment to you, with only faying, that

I am, Sir,

An ENGLISHMAN.

To the PRINTER.

LORD B. and his toad eater the D. of G. both knew the contents of Dr. Mufgrave's letter many weeks before it made its appearance. They had concerted many fchemes to fupprefs its publication ; but all thefe fchemes, however artfully managed, proved abortive. Lord B. who came frefh from the fchool of politics at Rome, embraced ftill the fame propenfity for abfolute monarchy as he did before he departed from England. He is grown, indeed, more cautious, more mafked, but not a jot lefs enterprifing. Foiled in his well-concealed attempts to prevent the publication of Dr. Mufgrave's letter, his next attempt was to render the publication of it inoperative and ineffectual. The difficulty lay in compaffing this defirable end. He knew very well that one ******** had married a
caft-

caft-off, who formerly held no mean rank in his toad eater's feraglio : this fame *********, his Lordfhip knew had been confidently intrufted at different times, with the moft important fecrets of Mr. Wilkes, the Chevalier D'Eon, and Lord Temple, and therefore the only fit perfon to be confidentially entrufted, as far as his Lordfhip might deem neceffary, with the opening a negociation for a treaty of union between the Earls of B--e, T----e, E------t, C-----m, Lord H-----d, and the petulant Duke of B------. Such a coalition, with his toad eater at the head, he rightly conceived, would be able to ftem any torrent of oppofition, were it to roll mountains high. But his Lordfhip, it will be feen, counted without his hoft. His firft intention was to difpatch ********* to Stow. This meafure could not be carried into execution but by another mode of application. ********* had already forfeited Lord T----e's confidence, but he did not care to acquaint either G. or B. with this fecret, which could not but be fatal to his own views; he therefore artfully declined going to Stow himfelf, adding, that the embaffy would have greater weight, and probably better fuccefs, was the D. of G. to wait in perfon on Lord T-----. ********* pretended to know the very bait that would tempt his Lordfhip ; it was nothing lefs than a Dukedom, and if he *********, was to make the offer, Lord T----e, he faid, might doubt the performance. By this device and advice of *********,

B. an l

B. and his toad eater were eafily betrayed into a fond belief of gaining over Lord T. to their faction. Accordingly, the D. of G. was pofted down to Stow, and this truly courtly vifit was immediately announced in every news-paper throughout the kingdom. The fuccefs of this vifit is no longer a myf-tery. The wild, incoherent, crude plan of operations, were conveyed, without lofs of time, to Fonthill, and from Fonthill it foon arrived at Plymouth. Dr. Mufgrave finding this once formidable and blood-thirfty fac-tion tottering, and failing of fupport from Lord T. thought it a glorious opportunity to crufh the whole junto, by hanging them out to public view and public odium. With this view, and to do juftice to a brave, but greatly injured people, the Doctor, with a courage not to be daunted, publifhed that well-timed letter, which has already unfilm'd the eyes of every fubject in the kingdom, and which, in a few days, will receive a further elucidation. from

The BRITISH SPY.

To the P R I N T E R.

IN my former letter I furnifhed your rea-ders with an anecdote relative to Mr. ********. This man, who is connected with his Grace the D. of G. by the apron-ftring tenure ;

tenure; the prefent modifh, and by much the ftrongeft of all holds, has been conftantly and moft fecretly employed for thefe laft fix weeks, as a go-between to the D. of G. and the Soi-difant l'Homme de Charactere, M. D'Eon.

To throw a veil over this myfterious negociation, and in order to blind the eyes of the prying public, the pretty Frenchman who lives in Petty France, has for this fortnight paft been roaring out in every coffeehoufe he frequents, that Mr. ********, the gobetween above-mentioned, has betrayed his moft facred fecrets to the D. of G. and the whole B-----d junto. This flimfy, gaufy device, was no fooner made public, but it was feen through by every tyro in politics. And the Frenchman was compelled by his new employers to lay afide the mafk. He was ordered by this new fett of mafters, who will always tyrannize over him in proportion to the penfion they give him : he was ordered I fay flatly to deny every circumftance in Dr. Mulgrave's patriotic letter, and boldly to affert, " that he never entered into any treaty " for the fale of his papers." Nothing is fo eafy to a Frenchman, efpecially if they have been once initiated into the diplomatic corps, as to affert one thing for another, where they know they cannot for the prefent moment be detected. But what will the good people of England think of the veracity of this fame Frenchman, when I call upon him in this public manner to declare for what
reafon,

reafon, at whofe inftigation, and for what valuable confideration in money, he fuppreffed the publication of *thofe three letters* relative to the late peace-makers ?

I know, Mr. Printer, I fpeak ænigmatically to the generality of your readers, when I talk of three letters. But the D. of B-----d underftands me ; Lord B--- underftands me ; and D'Eon, if he has any regard for truth, ought to blufh at the bare mention of thofe three letters. There is but one moral tie can bind a French gentlemen, that is, his word of honour. Let D'Eon then, if he dare, lay his hand upon his Croix de St. Louis, and fwear, upon his *honour*, that he never received directly or indirectly, without equivocation, or mental refervation, any money, penfion, emolument, or promife, for fuppreffing the publication of the three letters in queftion, and he fhall either be credited, or publickly confuted, by

The BRITISH SPY.

To the PRINTER.

DOCTOR MUSGRAVE's addrefs to the freeholders of the county of Devon, and the Chevalier D'Eon's anfwer to it, having engroffed the public attention, give me leave, firft, to confider the nature and tendency of the addrefs,

drefs, and then to make a few remarks on the Chevalier's anfwer.

Mr. Mufgrave has told us a feries of facts within his own knowledge, the authenticity of which are corroborated by the names of the parties concerned, and the periods in which they were tranfacted. He tells us, that Sir George Yonge, Mr. Fitzherbert, and other members of parliament, informed him at different times, that the Chevalier D'Eon was really to impeach three perfons of felling the peace to the French---that Sir George Yonge in particular told him, that he under-ftood the charge could be fupported by writ-ten as well as by living evidence. By the di-rection of Dr. Blackftone, Mr. Mufgrave went to Lord Halifax *on the* 10*th of May*, 1765, and delivered to him an exact narra-tive of the intelligence he had received at Pa-ris concerning the late peace, and at the fame time gave him copies of four letters to and from Lord Hertford. *On the* 17*th of May*, 1765, juft feven days after he delivered the narrative to Lord Halifax, Mr. Fitzherbert told the Doctor, that overtures were then making to the Chevalier D'Eon to get his papers from him for a ftipulated fum of mo-ney. Lord Halifax, although repeatedly preffed by Doctor Mufgrave to enquire into the truth of the charge, firft, objected to all public fteps that would lead to the truth, to avoid giving *an alarm*; and, at laft, abfo-folutely refufed to take any cognizance of it, either in private or public. Thus fruftrated

in

in every application to the fecretary of ftate,
the Doctor carried his papers to the Speaker,
who very readily allowed the expediency of
their being laid before the Houfe of Commons, but at the fame time peremptorily refufed to promote the enquiry.

This, Sir, is the fubftance of Dr. Mufgrave's addrefs, which carries with it fuch a
face of authenticity, that nothing but a public inveftigation of the facts can exculpate
the parties concerned. As to the tendency of
it, every unprejudiced reader muft allow, that
the public good, and not an inclination to ag-
gravate the guilt of any particular perfon, was
his object.

If the allegations contained in the addrefs
are not fairly ftated---if Doctor Mufgrave has
been guilty of injuring private characters,
and of impofing falfhoods on the public---
why, in God's name, is he not contradicted?
---Why do not the accufed exculpate themfelves?---Why are not the public unde-
ceived?---Why fhould *they* be filent whofe
conduct is principally arraigned, and a vindication, fuch as it is, be publifhed by a man,
whofe veracity in this refpect is by no means
to be relied on? For when his papers were
purchafed from him, the condition of the
obligation no doubt was, that their contents
fhould be buried in oblivion.

When the official conduct of a fecretary of
ftate, or of any other fervant of the crown, is
arraigned, the public have an undoubted
right to be fatisfied either of their guilt or

innocence, in order that the law of the land
may in either cafe take effect. When the
character of an honeft man is unjuftly and
publicly attacked, he will not poftpone the
vindication of his innocence until a legal enquiry can be fet on foot in a court of law;
he ought to exculpate himfelf through the
fame channel he has been accufed. Therefore, until Doctor Blackftone tells us the con-
verfation that paffed between him and Mr.
Mufgrave, previous to his waiting on Lord
Halifax---Until Lord Halifax informs us
whether Doctor Mufgrave did or did not de-
liver to him a narrative of the intelligence he
had received at Paris, concerning the peace
in 1764, and likewife publifh the copies of
the four letters to and from Lord Hertford;
which, as they are of a public nature, his
politenefs need not ftumble at --- Until Sir
George Yonge and Mr. Fitzherbert publicly
deny every circumftance relative to their feveral converfations with Doctor Mufgrave,
efpecially what paffed between Mr. Fitzherbert and him *on the 17th day of May, 1765*---
And until the Speaker acquaints us with the
reafon why he allowed the expediency of lay-
ing thefe important papers before the Houfe
of Commons, and at the fame time *refufed to
promote the enquiry*---Until all thefe matters
are promulged and fufficiently authenticated,
the impartial and difpaffionate part of man-
kind muft and will give credit to the facts
contained in the addrefs.

I come

I come now, Sir, to make a few remarks
on the Chevalier D'Eon's anfwer, which I
fhall do with the fame impartiality I have
confidered the addrefs, and leave the public
to draw the line between the honeft fincerity
of the Englifhman, and the evafive *fineffe* of
the Frenchman.

Monfieur le Chevalier, notwithftanding
his long refidence in England, and the efteem
and friendfhip he is favoured with from *fome*
of the inhabitants (the reafon of which he
knows beft) ftill preferves his *native* infince-
rity and politenefs. His letter to Dr. Mufgrave is as foreign to the purpofe of an anfwer to the addrefs, as the conduct of our prefent miniftry in fuffering his mafter, the Grand
Monarque, to conquer Corfica, was foreign
to the faith of treaty, and repugnant to the
intereft of this kingdom---than which no
two pofitions can be more oppofite.

The Chevalier has very *politely* paffed fome
French compliments on the doctor's oratory
and patriotifm---has talked a good deal of his
own integrity and zeal for truth---blames
him for naming a perfon of his *vaft* confequence in fo public a manner, and manfully
denies every circumftance he is publicly
known to have been concerned in at the time
mentioned in the addrefs. But what does all
this amount to with refpect to Mr. Mufgrave's
allegations? He, indeed, very juftly fays, that
the evidence of the Chevalier would have
been decifive at the time he urged Lord Halifax to fend for him to examine him, and to
perufe

peruse his papers which he *then* had in his poffeffion; but in his addrefs to the free-holders of Devon, he neither defires nor ex-pects any proofs from him *now*, becaufe he either knows, or fhrewdly fufpects, that no written evidence is now to be found in his cuftody.

The Chevalier defires to know the perfon or perfons in this country, who would have prefumed to make an overture to him for the fale of his papers---I wifh to God I could tell him!---or rather that I could tell the public---for the Chevalier himfelf, I dare fay, wants no information in that affair. It is much to be wifhed, however, that Lord Halifax or the Speaker had examined the Chevalier, and that it might at leaft have been known what fum was paid by England, and for what confideration it was given to France, at the conclufion of the laft ever memorable and glorious peace.

TULLIUS.

LETTER I.

To Dr. MUSGRAVE, of PLYMOUTH.

SIR,

THE meritorious and intrepid manner in which you have ftepped forth, and called the public attention to the negociation

of

of the laſt infamous peace, deſerves the thanks
and applauſe of your country. As an individual of this country, not wholly unacquainted with ſome parts of that negociation, you have my poor thanks : but thanks
alone are not ſufficient in ſuch a cauſe; I
ſhould hold myſelf the baſeſt of Engliſhmen,
if I did not contribute my mite towards ac-
compliſhing a full and impartial enquiry
into the manner in which that important
work was conducted. Such parts of the negociation as have accidentally come to my knowledge, I ſhall freely relate. If my account
is true, as I have great reaſon to believe it is
in general, I hope it will warm ſome virtuous
man to ſtand up in his place, and call for the
papers relating to that negociation. In a
pamphlet, intituled, *The preſent State of the
Nation*, &c. p. 24, 8vo. edit. publiſhed laſt
winter, there is this extraordinary paſſage,
evidently alluding to theſe papers, which
I have often wondered was not taken no-
tice of; " Whether by the treaty Great
" Britain obtained all that ſhe might have
" obtained, is a queſtion to which thoſe only
" who were acquainted with the ſecrets of
" the French and Spaniſh cabinets can give
" an anſwer. *The correſpondence relative to
" that negociation has not been laid before the
" public*; for the laſt parliament approved of
" the peace as it was, without thinking it
" neceſſary to enquire whether better terms
" might not have been had."
The ſecret of the negociation, or ultimatum, on the part of England, was neither in
the

the D. of B. the B. A. at Paris ; nor in the late Earl of Egremont, the *official* minister at home, who was Secretary of State for the Southern department ; but between Lord Bute and the Sardinian Minister in London, and the Duc de Choifeul and the Sardinian Minister at Paris.

The fact, of thus committing the management of the most important affairs of Great Britain to the Ministers of a foreign power, is extraordinary and alarming, and ought to be confidered as highly criminal ; efpecially when we recollect, that the Sardinian Minister in London, at the time of his prefent Majefty's coronation, figned a proteft in favour of the Houfe of Savoy, which he procured to be legally attefted and given in, in the name of the King his mafter. He printed, or caufed to be printed, ' the *Ge-* ' *nealogie de la Famille Royale d'Angleterre*, by ' which he hoped, at a future day, that the ' ridiculous claims of his mafter's family, as ' being, although Papifts, immediately def- ' cended from Henrietta Maria, the daugh- ' ter of Charles I. would have prevailed ' over thofe of the Houfe of Brunfwick, ' who are defcended from Elizabeth, Elec- ' trefs Palatine, one degree more remote ' from the crown, as being the daughter of ' James I. He might hope for a general ' confufion among us ; but being born un- ' der arbitrary government, he could not ' have the leaft idea of the only lawful right ' to the crown of thefe realms, a parliamen-

' tary

' tary right. The contrary doctrine was in
' Queen Anne's time exprefsly declared to
' be *high treafon* by a particular ftatute, the
" Act for the better fecuring her Majefty's
" perfon and government, and of the fuc-
" ceffion to the crown of England in the
" Proteftant line ;" ' *That if any perfon or*
' *perfons, from and after the 25th day of March,*
' *1706, fhall malicioufly, advifedly and directly,*
' *by writing or printing, declare, maintain, or*
' *affirm that the Kings or Queens of England, with*
' *and by the authority of the parliament of Eng-*
' *land, are not able to make laws and ftatutes of*
' *fufficient force and validity to limit and bind the*
' *crown of this realm, and the* DESCENT, LIMI-
' TATION, INHERITANCE, *and government*
' *thereof, every fuch perfon or perfons fhall be*
' *guilty of High Treafon, and being thereof con-*
' *victed and attainted, &c. &c.* Count Viri
' acted by the exprefs orders of his Court,
' in conjuction with the Court of France.
' In the fame manner the two Courts acted
' in concert at the beginning of this century,
' in the laft year of our glorious Deliverer,
' King William III. Count Maffei, the Am-
' baffador from Savoy, delivered in the firft
' famous proteftation, in the name of the
' Duchefs of Savoy, againft the Hanover fuc-
' ceffion, at the time the Duke himfelf com-
' manded the French army in Italy, with
' Marfhal Catinat and the Prince of Vaude-
' mont under him, and every action of his
' life was dictated by France.'

The

The prefent Count V. (who, during his late father's life time, was known by the name of M. De Verois) had a penfion granted him for his fervices in this negociation of 1000l. per ann. on the Irifh eftablifhment, though not in his own name. In the *debates relative to the affairs of Ireland, in the years* 1763 *and* 1764, &c. *infcribed by permiffion to Lord Chatham*, we find this fact mentioned, Vol. II. page 475, by Mr. Edmund Sexton Perry, who thus fpeaks :
" I fhall communicate a fact to this Houfe.
" There is a penfion granted nominally to
" one George Charles, but really to Mon-
" fieur De Verois, the Sardinian Minifter,
" for negociating the peace that has juft been
" concluded with the Minifter of France.
" I muft confefs, Sir, that, in my opinion,
" this fervice deferved no fuch recompence,
" at leaft on our part. If it is thought a
" defenfible meafure, I fhould be glad to
" know, why it was not avowed; and why,
" if it is proper we fhould pay 1000l. a
" year to Monf. De Verois, we fhould be
" made to believe that we pay it to George
" Charles."
Befides the above penfion, there was certainly a remittance from France or Spain, or both, of a confiderable fum of money; but for whom it was defigned is not at prefent fo certainly known. However, there is no doubt that Count V. is thoroughly acquainted with the whole of this tranfaction : but now that the affair of the peace begins to

be

be enquired into, he is preparing to depart the kingdom; and has actually fold his penfion upon the Irifh Eftablifhment for 16000l, or thereabouts.

When the D. of B. fet out for aris, which was on the 5th of September, 1762, he had *full powers* to treat with the French miniftry upon the terms of peace. But when he arrived at Calais, a meffenger was difpatched after him, containing a limitation of thofe powers. Upon which, he inftantly difpatched the fame meffenger back to London, declaring (by letter) he would proceed no further, unlefs his former inftructions were reftored. He waited at Calais for the return of this meffenger, who brought a reftoration of his former inftructions. However, he fubmitted, notwithftanding this affected fpirit, to fee the conquefts of a glorious war bargained for and furrendered by the two Sardinian minifters. In a word, the D. made no important figure in the negociation, till an an event turned up, which feemed, by the confufion it occafioned, to be totally unexpected. This was the capture of the Havannah.

This being only an introductory letter, my next, I hope, will be more worthy of your attention; at leaft, it will contain fome important truths. I am, Sir,

Your moft humble fervant,

An ENGLISHMAN.

LETTER

LETTER II.

To Dr. MUSGRAVE of PLYMOUTH.

SIR,

MY laſt letter concluded with the mention of the conqueſt of the Havannah. The news of this important conqueſt arrived in England on the 29th of September, 1762, while the treaty of peace was negociating. Until this period, the D. of B---- had little or no trouble in the negocitien, for the principle articles or great outlines of the terms of peace had been previouſly ſettled between Lord Bute and Monſ. De Verois (now Count Viry) in England, and and the Duc de Choiſeul and the Sardinian miniſter at Paris.

At this time the Right Hon. G--- G---- was Secretary of State for the Northern department, and by his office (being a commoner) was to carry the peace through the Houſe of Commons, when it ſhould be laid before the Houſe. When the news of the conqueſt of the Havannah came, and it was directly determined by the Favourite to give up this important iſland, becauſe it ſhould not embarraſs the negociation, nor impede the concluſion of the peace, Mr. G----- differed, and, in particular, inſiſted upon an indemnification for it, from either France or Spain. He wanted St. Lucia and Porto Rico,

or

or the entire property of Jucatan and Florida.
The Favourite refused to make application
for any of these; upon which Mr. G-----
resigned October 12, 1762 †. Mr. Fox (now
Lord Holland) was then called upon to carry
the peace through the House of Commons.
Lord Halifax succeeded to Mr. G-----'s office. But Lord Egremont, being of Mr.
G-----'s opinion, prevailed to have an in-
struction sent to the D. of B----- to demand
Florida only, which was granted without he-
sitation; for the messenger who was dis-
patched to the Duke at Paris with this demand, returned in eight days, with an account of its having been complied with. The
fact is, the French minister (Choiseul) obliged the Spanish minister to agree to this

---

† In the pamphlet, intituled, *An Appendix to the State
of the Nation*, we find this fact strongly pointed at, p. 16.
wherein the author says, in reply to the *Observer*: " If
" he means to charge the great statesman (Mr. G.) who
" was Secretary of State at the time the plans for the re-
" duction of Martinique and the Havannah were carried
" into execution, with consenting to restore them *without*
" *compensation*; I must tell him, that it was publicly
" spoken of, at the time the treaty of Paris was negociat-
" ing, that this gentleman resigned his office of Secre-
" tary of State for no other reason, *than that further cef-*
" *sions in the West Indies were not insisted on.*" And in the
Observations on the State of the Nation, we find that
author not unacquainted with this part of the negociation,
though, agreeable to the principles of the party he es-
pouses, it is but faintly touched; page 29, 8vo edit. are
these words, " If this gentleman's hero of finance, in-
" stead of flying from the treaty, which, though he now
" defends, *he could not approve*, and would not oppose; if
" he, instead of shifting into an office, *which removed him*
" *from the manufacture of the treaty*," &c.

demand,

demand, without fending to his court. A proof of the difcretionary power which was vefted in the French minifter by the court of Spain, to agree to whatever compenfation fhould be infifted upon for the Havannah.

The following anecdote concerning the Englifh Ultimatum may throw fome light on the preceding fact:---Towards the latter end of the negociation, Mr. Wood, then Secretary to Lord Egremont, called one day at the Duc de Nivernois's (the French Ambaffador in London) about three o'clock, and defired to fpeak with him. The Swifs told Mr. Wood, his Excellency was dreffing, and could not be difturbed : but Mr. Wood infifting upon admittance, was carried up ftairs, and paffing through a bed-chamber leading to the dreffing room, he laid fome papers upon the bed, and covered them with his hat. This circumftance being obferved by the French Secretary, he directly whifpered the Ambaffador to keep Mr. Wood to dinner, and he would copy the papers if they contained any thing effential. This was accordingly done : and thefe very papers, which contained nothing lefs than the Ultimatum on the part of England, were actually copied by the French Secretary and his clerks, and difpatched that very night to the Duc de Choifeul at Paris. Thus the French Minifter at Paris was in poffeffion of thefe important papers at leaft two days before the D. of B-----.

In

In a fubfequent conference which the D.
of B------ had with the French Minifter, he
urged a compliance to his demands in a high
and preremptory tone ; the wily French Minifter fmiled, and told his G. *He knew the
fentiments of the court of London upon the whole
bufinefs.*

It was the current report in England, when
the D. of B------ returned from France, that
he had frequently faid to his friends, that he
could have obtained better terms of peace if
he had been permitted. If he was controuled,
why does he not now fhew thofe inftances of
controul, and who it was that obliged him
to facrifice the conquefts of the war ? As he
is known to keep a diary of all public tranfactions wherein he is concerned, there is no
doubt of his being able to give full information ; and as days and dates are fometimes of
importance in affairs of this kind, his diary
will affift him greatly on this occafion. Befides, his letters are fomewhere in exiftence ;
the Chevalier D'Eon never faw them, and
confequently a motion in the H--- of C----
might produce them. We fhould then fee
who were the betrayers of our country in that
infamous peace : And who it was that fo frequently preffed his G. to conclude the negociation, and fign the treaty. The originals
of all thefe important letters are ftill in
being ; and if they fhould not, there is no
doubt the D. has a copy of them in his diary.
I repeat it emphatically, the correfpondence
relative to the negociation ought to be laid
before

before the public. The Commons of England have a right to call for it; and it is a duty which they owe to their country and to posterity.

Whether the immediate ceffion of Florida, or what other caufe that has not yet tranf-pired, encouraged the demand of Porto Rico, or whether the D. of B. knowing Mr. G---'s fentiments, made that demand himfelf, finding Florida fo eafily given up ; certain it is, that a demand of that important ifland was made ; and here the French Minifter reforted to his chicane. A meffenger was fent with this demand to the Court of Madrid. Fourteen days were allowed for the meffenger to return. During this interval, the D. received exprefs and pofitive orders *to fign the treaty immediately.* Two days after the treaty was figned, and within the fourteen days, the meffenger returned from Madrid, with the furrender of the ifland. It has been fuf-pected, perhaps from the complexion of the fact, that the ifland was purchafed. If it was, Count V. no doubt, knows both the fum that was given, and to whom it was con-figned. If any fum actually was given, it was by Spain ; for the view of France was, to make Spain pay the piper.

My next will contain fome further particulars of this extraordinary negociaaion.

I am, Sir,

Your humble fervant,

An ENGLISHMAN.

LETTER

LETTER III.

To Dr. MUSGRAVE of Plymouth.

SIR,

THE article refpecting the Eaft-India
Company, is a demonftration that
better terms of peace might have been obtained, if they had been infifted upon. During the negociation Mr. Wood waited upon
Mr. Rous, on the fubject of an article, in-
cluding the Company's affairs, to be inferted
in the treaty. An article was accordingly
framed, and fent to the minifters, who faid
it was impoffible to obtain what was therein
demanded. They altered it : and if it had
been permitted to remain with their altera-
tions, as it had been agreed to by the French
minifters, and as it ftood in the prelimina-
ries, the interefts of the Company would
have been effentially injured. But Lord
Clive oppofed it; and in confequence of this
oppofition, it was altered to the form in
which it now ftands in the general treaty.

With regard to the *prefent*, or rather *new*
treaty of commerce, the following is not a
little curious.

When the D. of B. Mr. N----le, and the
Ducs de Choifeul and Praflin were togethe:
at Choifeul's hotel, at a conference on the
peace, the D. of B. faid, he would not renew
the treaty of Commerce that was made at

Utrecht,

Utrecht, becaufe fome of the articles had
been objected to by the Britifh parliament.
The fubject dropped after a fhort converfa-
tion upon it: and they proceeded to renew
the treaty of Aix la Chapelle, and other matters. At length the D. of B. renewed the
fubject of the treaty of commerce: upon
which Choifeul faid, the treaty of commerce
had never been mentioned during the negociation. But, anfwered the D. it has always
been underftood. Choifeul replied, you
muft either take the treaty of commerce as it
now is, between the two nations (meaning
that which was offered to be renewed) or
there muft be no treaty of commerce at all.
The D. of B. declared, he would not accept
of that treaty; nor would he fign the treaty
of peace unlefs a treaty of commerce was pre-
vioufly agreed to. And fo, fays Choifeul,
you want to carve that treaty juft as you
pleafe; to put in fome articles, and to ftrike
out others---*No!* faid he in an exclamation,
and turning about to a picture of the French
King, which hung up in the room, and
clafping his hands together, cried out, *My
dear mafter! when I facrifice your honour, take
off my head.*

Mr. N----le then faid, Monf. Choifeul,
what better would you be if that treaty was
renewed? The Britifh parliament would dif-
approve of it, and the D. of B. would be
impeached for it.---Think you fo, faid Choifeul?---Yes, anfwered the D. of B. and added, if you do not confent to the making a

new

new treaty of commerce, I will return to England to-morrow morning, and tell the K. there is no honour in the French mini-ftry; that he muft fend for Mr. PITT, who is the only man to deal with them, and renew the war. The name of *Pitt* frightened the French minifter; he gave up the conteft. A treaty of commerce was made; but has. not been publifhed, nor was it laid before parliament.

During the negociation, the Duc de Choi-feul was conftantly complaining of the Eng-lifh news-papers; which, he faid, were con-tinually publifhing the terms of the peace; and thefe papers coming into France, he added, induced the French to think, and fay, he was facrificing the intereft of France in that treaty; which he apprehended might occafion fome enthufiaft to affaffinate him. In complai-fance to him, and to quiet his fears on that head, it was, that no authentic defence or even authentic account of the negociation and treaty, was ever publifhed.

Every reader will make his own obferva-tions on this feries of *extraordinary* FACTS. I have given them to the world without any of thofe advantages which they might have derived from a detail in fine language, being convinced, *that plain truth needs no flowers of fpeech.* I am, SIR,

Your moft humble fervant,

An ENGLISHMAN.

.